Follow the PROPHET

Sharing Time Activities
for Children

Written by Christena C. Nelson • Illustrated by Brenda S. Braun

EAGLE
GATE™

Salt Lake City, Utah

CCN: To Julie Gilbert Rapp (1970–1999)
I'm still your friend.
God be with you until we meet again.

BSB: To William L. and Loa Dean Sorensen,
who taught me to follow the prophet.
And to my love, Barry Braun,
who keeps me on track.

Contents

Preface

"Surely the Lord God will do nothing, until he revealeth his secret unto his servants the prophets" (JST—Amos 3:7). Because the will of the Lord is made known through his prophets, it is crucial that children learn while they are young to follow the prophet. Parents, leaders, and teachers play an important role in that learning process, and this activity book will help them teach children of the blessings that come from following the prophet.

These easy-to-prepare presentations are designed to complement the 2001 Primary Children's Sacrament Meeting Presentation, "Follow the Prophet." They are appropriate for use in sharing time and Primary classes as well as in family home evenings and Sunday learning times. Many of them are simple enough to be presented effectively by older children. For ease of use in a family setting, you may wish to photocopy or print out all the illustrations at once and keep them in a file so that a child could choose from among available materials. Older children may also be able to use the included CD-ROM themselves to create and color artwork.

This book provides a variety of learning activities to help maximize teaching opportunities. From flannel-board stories to noncompetitive games, coloring booklets to role-playing situations, these activities are designed to involve children directly and effectively.

You may print out, photocopy, trace, enlarge, or otherwise reproduce the materials in this book for personal use at home or in the classroom (not for distribution). All illustrations in this book are included on the CD and can be sized, copied, and exported to a program such as Microsoft Paint for coloring. To install the art, insert the CD-ROM in the appropriate drive and follow the on-screen instructions. Feel free to use your creativity in adapting any of the ideas and concepts in this book. We hope you will find them a valuable resource in your important work of helping children follow the prophet.

1
What Is a Prophet?

PREPARATION: Print out or photocopy, color, and cut out the flannel board figures. Make a printout or copy of the acrostic handout for each child. For older children, use the handout that includes only the seven vertical letters (image 1-1). For younger children, use the handout that includes the whole verse (image 1-1b). Cut out the corresponding pictures. Have ready a flannel board and chalkboard, chalk, eraser, and glue sticks. (Bring pencils for the older children.) Draw a large version of the handout on a chalkboard.

PRESENTATION: Using the flannel board figures, relate the following analogy:

Mr. Sparks had a beautiful garden. He worked very hard to plant vegetables and fruit trees. Every day he would water the rows of beets, carrots, onions, squash, and tomatoes. Every week he trimmed the grapevines and fruit trees and pulled up the weeds. Every other week he fertilized. He watched for signs of rabbits or insects chewing on the leaves. Mr. Sparks worked so hard that sometimes he got blisters on his hands. He got hot and sweaty. But he didn't mind. He loved his garden.

In the middle of the summer, Mr. Sparks needed to go away for six weeks. What would

happen to his garden if no one took care of it for six weeks? What could Mr. Sparks do?

He had worked too hard to let his fruits and vegetables die. He asked his friend Mr. Garcia to tend his garden. He knew he could trust him. He gave Mr. Garcia all the tools he would need.

Mr. Garcia also loved gardening. He followed Mr. Spark's instructions: every day he watered, every week he trimmed trees and pulled weeds, every other week he fertilized. He kept the plants safe from insects and animals.

When Mr. Sparks returned, he found that his little plants had grown large and strong. He hugged Mr. Garcia. "Thank you for taking care of my garden!" he said. "I couldn't have done it better myself."

Heavenly Father and Jesus love us much more than Mr. Sparks loved his garden. Jesus worked hard to be our Savior. He showed us the way to live. He suffered for our pains and sins. Then he needed to go back to his Father. But who would take care of us while our Savior was away? Who would make sure that we would continue to grow strong until Jesus returned?

Heavenly Father and Jesus did not leave us alone. They gave us a prophet. The prophet follows all of Jesus' instructions. He works very hard to help people live the gospel. He teaches them about Heavenly Father and Jesus. He warns them of danger. He prepares them for the Master Gardener's return. The prophet is a friend God can trust.

ACTIVITY: Distribute the handouts and glue sticks (and a pencil for the older children). Using the drawing on the chalkboard, explain that an acrostic poem uses the first or last letter of each line in the poem to spell out a word or to make a string of letters in an alphabet. Acrostic poetry is used in the Bible.

Ask the children: "If you were to write an acrostic verse about a prophet, what words would you use to describe what a prophet does?" Have the older children suggest sentences that start with the letters *P, R, O, P, H, E,* or *T,* and write them by the corresponding letter. Help younger children come up with words that are similar to the ones on the handouts. Distribute the seven small pictures to each child and ask them to glue the corresponding picture by each sentence. Use the pictures to explain the words.

President of the Church

Revealer of God's will

Obedient example

Predictor of future events

Holder of all priesthood keys

Experienced in service

Testifier of Jesus Christ

Image 1-1a

PRESIDENT OF THE CHURCH

President Spencer W. Kimball called many more missionaries to preach the gospel throughout the world.

REVEALER OF GOD'S WILL

Moses gave his people the Ten Commandments.

OBEDIENT EXAMPLE

Abraham was willing to obey the Lord's command to sacrifice his son Isaac.

PREDICTOR OF FUTURE EVENTS

Noah warned his people of the Flood.

HOLDER OF ALL PRIESTHOOD KEYS

Peter, James, and John restored the Melchizedek Priesthood to the earth when they blessed Joseph Smith and gave him priesthood keys.

EXPERIENCED IN SERVICE

King Benjamin served his people.

TESTIFIER OF JESUS CHRIST

Isaiah prophesied of Jesus' birth.

Image 1-1b

Image 1-1c

Image 1-4

Image 1-3

Image 1-2

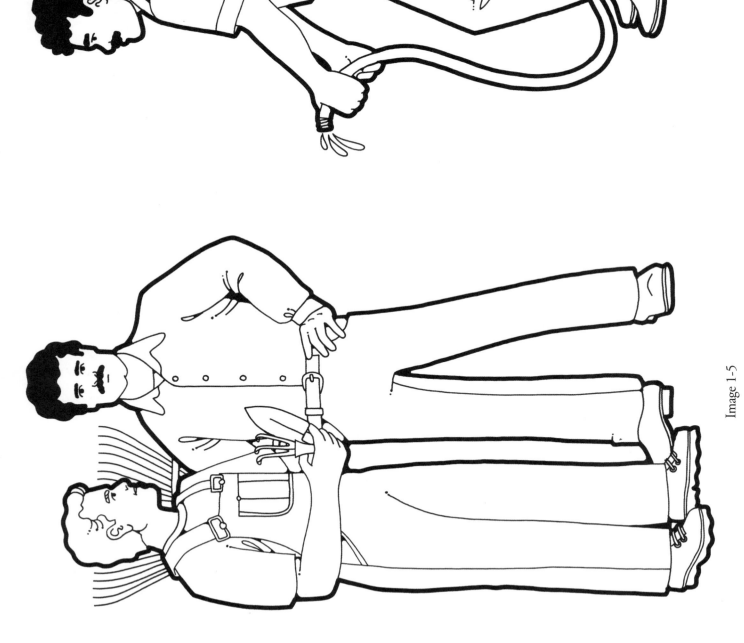

Image 1-6

Image 1-5

2

The Prophet Is the President of The Church of Jesus Christ of Latter-day Saints

PREPARATION: Put the following objects in a bag or a pillowcase: a model or toy airplane, a conductor's baton or instrument, a jar of candy, a toy sheep. Bring a crayon or pencil for each child. Print out or photocopy and color the pictures of Jesus ordaining Peter and of the latter-day prophets. Make one copy of the worksheet for each child.

PRESENTATION: Call on children to pull out one object at a time from the pillowcase. Pose the corresponding questions to the whole group:

Imagine a jet airliner that is loaded with passengers, but has no pilot.

Would the plane be able to take off?

Would the people reach their destination?

Imagine an orchestra without a conductor.

Would the musicians know when to start playing their instruments?

How might the music sound?

Imagine a candy store with no manager.

Who would work there?

How would they know what time to come to work?

Imagine a flock of sheep with no shepherd.

How would they find water?

Would they be safe from wolves?

Now imagine a plane with *two* pilots. One wants to fly the plane to the northeast; the other wants to go northwest.

Imagine an orchestra with *three* conductors. The first wants to play the music fast; the second wants to play slowly; the third wants to play an entirely different song.

Imagine a candy store with *two* managers. The first orders a huge shipment of taffy; the second also orders a huge shipment of taffy.

Imagine a flock of sheep with *five* shepherds. Each shepherd thinks he knows the best pastures. They each set off in different directions to tend the flock.

Groups of people and organizations need one person to be their leader and unite and direct them under one purpose. There might be other leaders to help out, but even those leaders have to answer to one main leader. Having more than one person in charge can be almost as confusing as having no leader at all.

(Hold up picture of Peter's ordination.)

Jesus knew that the early members of the Church would need someone to be in charge after he returned to be with his Father. He prepared the Apostle Peter for that job. After Jesus returned to be with Heavenly Father, Peter became President of the Church. Peter received directions from the Lord, so Jesus was still leading the Church through Peter.

Who is the President of our Church today? How does he receive directions? Just like Peter, our prophet today is instructed by the Lord. Jesus still leads the Church today, but he does so through President Gordon B. Hinckley.

Does the President have helpers? Yes, all of us help him by doing our jobs in the Church. Can our bishop or branch president receive a revelation for the whole Church? No, only the prophet can do that. The bishop or branch president receives revelation for his own ward or branch. Can our Primary president make an announcement for the whole Church? No, only for her own Primary.

ACTIVITY: Use the pictures to tell the stories of various latter-day prophets and of their directions to Church members. Urge the children to listen well, since they will be doing a worksheet afterward. At the end of each story, have the children tell you out loud or role-play what they have done to obey these prophets' commands.

The prophet Brigham Young asked the Saints to move west, so they could be safe and prosper. He asked them to sell their homes and furniture and take with them only the essentials. If you

had been a member of the Church then, what would you have done?

President Gordon B. Hinckley asked Latter-day Saints to help the Church save money by taking turns cleaning our church buildings. When it is your family's turn to clean up, what will you do?

President Lorenzo Snow asked the Saints to pay a full tithing. What will you do with your money?

President Spencer W. Kimball told Latter-day Saints to plant a garden. If you had been a Church member when President Kimball was the prophet, what would you have done?

President Ezra Taft Benson told Church members that God was not pleased with them because they had not been reading and using the Book of Mormon enough. What did the righteous Latter-day Saints at that time do?

The prophet Howard W. Hunter asked Latter-day Saints to make the temple a symbol of their membership in the Church. How can you do this?

Distribute the worksheets and pencils. Ask the children to look at the prophet illustrated on the left, and match the revelation that he received by choosing it from the pictures on the right. Encourage them to share with their families what they learned about each prophet.

President Gordon B. Hinckley

President Howard W. Hunter

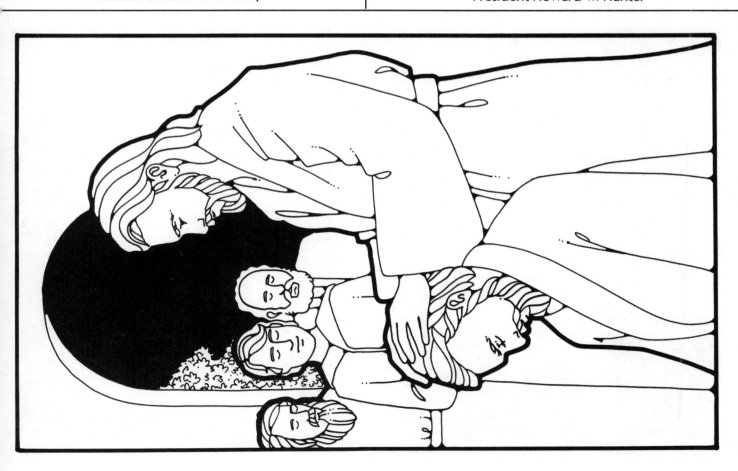

President Brigham Young

President Spencer W. Kimball

President Ezra Taft Benson

President Lorenzo Snow

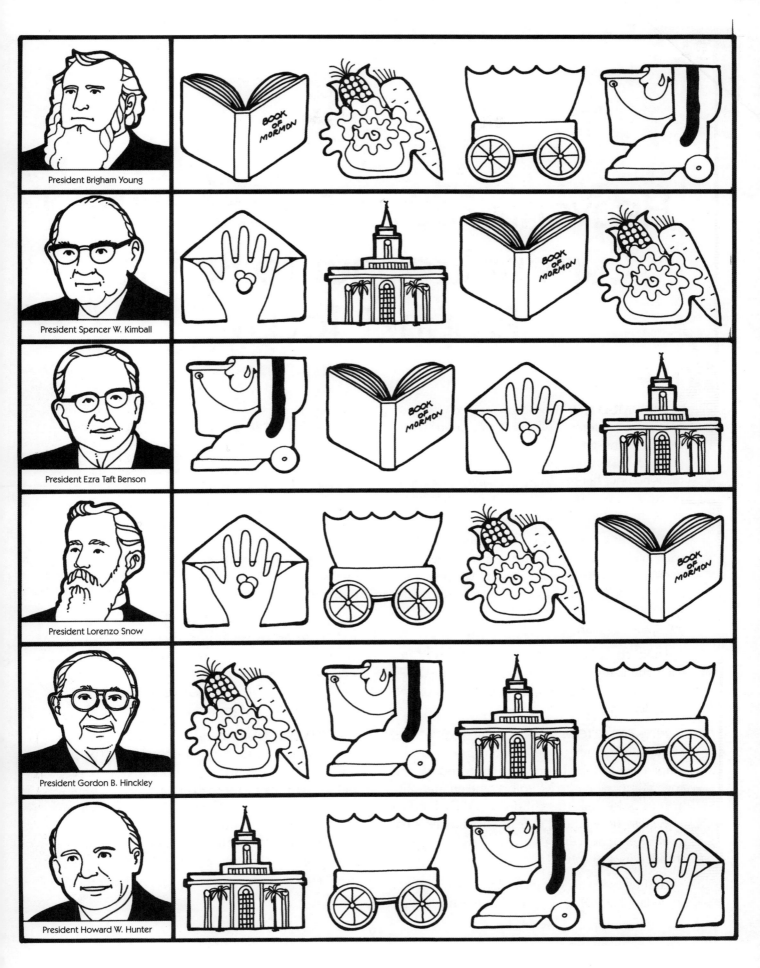

President Brigham Young

President Spencer W. Kimball

President Ezra Taft Benson

President Lorenzo Snow

President Gordon B. Hinckley

President Howard W. Hunter

Image 2-8

3

Heavenly Father Prepared the Current Prophet to Be the Prophet Today

PREPARATION: Invite an "expert" guest (a musician, athlete, physician) to attend. If, for example, the guest is a flute player, ask her to perform a short piece. Then have her share information about her teachers, how much she had to practice, where she attended school, competitions she entered, work experience, and so on.

Print out or photocopy the "Prophet's Pathway" on two overhead transparencies. Set up the overhead projector with a screen. (If this equipment is not available to you, enlarge the "Pathway" to poster size.) You will need a transparency marker.

Make copies of the two-paged "Pathway" for each child. Tape the pages together on the back, making sure they line up. Bring crayons or colored pencils.

PRESENTATION: Introduce the "expert" and invite him or her to deliver the presentation. Emphasize to the children the time and experience that person needed to become an authority in that field. Ask the children: "What kind of 'specialist' do we need to lead our church? What kind of experience does a man need before he is called as a prophet?"

God knows who will grow up to be a prophet someday. He makes sure the future prophet has the experiences he will need to be President of the Church. The Lord prepared Gordon B. Hinckley to be a prophet in our time.

Display the "Prophet's Pathway." Use a marker to draw a line from picture to picture and show the path that President Hinckley took to reach the point he is at today. Ask the children to tell you which order to follow. (Tell them, for example, that he did not jump from childhood to ordination as a General Authority. He matured through each step of the process.)

Emphasize that he has spent more than seventy-seven years in Church service, the majority of those years as a General Authority. He was well prepared to be the prophet. He still works very hard trying to help people be happier. We should pray for our prophet.

ACTIVITY: Distribute the "Pathways" to the children and invite them to draw a line (path) from picture to picture in chronological order and to color the pictures. (The pictures are numbered chronologically to help children draw the path.) Encourage them to follow a righteous path. Remind them that a Primary child alive today might be a future prophet!

12

The Prophet's Pathway

1. President Hinckley's grandparents made many sacrifices as early pioneers.

2. President Hinckley was born on June 23, 1910, to loving parents who named him Gordon Bitner Hinkley.

3. Gordon was a small, sickly child. He suffered from asthma, allergies, and many earaches. When he was two, he became very ill from whooping cough.

12. His testimony grew as he learned about the Savior while reading the scriptures on his mission in England (1933–35).

10. In high school, Gordon loved reading the books in his family's library.

11. He graduated from the University of Utah in June 1932 and became a good writer.

13. He married Marjorie Pay in the Salt Lake Temple in 1937.

15. He served in the Sunday School organization and in stake presidencies.

14. He and his wife raised a family.

22. He became the President of the Church in March 1995.

21. President Spencer W. Kimball called him to be a counselor in the First Presidency in July 1981. In November 1985, President Ezra Taft Benson called him as a counselor. Then, in June 1994, President Howard W. Hunter called him as a counselor.

Image 3-1

4. When Gordon was about five, his ear hurt very badly. His father gave him a priesthood blessing and then put a warm bag of salt on his ear. Gordon's pain left, and he fell asleep in his father's arms.

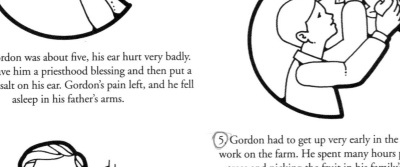

5. Gordon had to get up very early in the morning to work on the farm. He spent many hours pruning the trees and picking the fruit in his family's orchard.

6. When President Joseph F. Smith announced that Church members should save one night each week to be with family, the Hinckleys began holding family home evening. During family home evening, Gordon's father told inspiring stories, and the children performed.

9. Shortly after Gordon became a deacon, he attended a stake priesthood meeting. As the congregation stood and sang a song about Joseph Smith, a powerful spiritual feeling entered Gordon's heart, witnessing that Joseph Smith was a true prophet of God.

8. Gordon was baptized by his father in 1919.

7. He felt safe and peaceful after saying his prayers at night.

16. He served as secretary to the Missionary Executive Committee of the Church.

18. He supervised the Far East Missions of the Church.

20. He traveled all over the world, dedicating countries to the gospel, creating new stakes, assisting at temple dedications, and attending area conferences.

17. He helped prepare the temple endowment in many different languages for the Swiss Temple.

19. He was sustained as an Assistant to the Quorum of the Twelve Apostles on April 6, 1958, and was called as an Apostle on September 30, 1961.

4

What Has Heavenly Father Told Us through Our Prophet at This General Conference?

PREPARATION: Using a square-shaped piece of heavy cardboard, make a television frame large enough for a child's head to fit inside it. Cut out a square opening in the TV. Make a microphone by forming a ball with aluminum foil and placing it atop a cardboard tube from a roll of paper towels. Wrap the entire tube and attached ball with foil.

Carefully watch general conference, taking notes on the prophet's and his counselors' messages. Use those notes to prompt the children in the lesson below. You may also want to send home notes with the children the week before conference asking them to listen carefully to the prophet's messages.

Print out or photocopy a "First Presidency Page" for each child, plus two extras. Gather crayons.

Make a "Conference Cube":

1. Cut out the six extra pictures of the First Presidency.

2. Find a small cube-shaped box. Or make your own.

3. Cover the box with butcher paper or wrapping paper.

4. Glue one of the First Presidency pictures to each of the six sides.

PRESENTATION: Ask the children, "Who watched conference? Can you remember any of the messages that were delivered by the prophet or his counselors?" (Let the children name as many as they can remember.)

Invite the children to "report" on some of those messages.

Have several children come to the front of the room, hold the microphone, and look through the screen. They should pretend to be a news reporter, and deliver a brief report of that individual's talk in conference.

ACTIVITY: Distribute the "First Presidency Pages" and crayons. Ask the children to draw a picture under each presidency member, depicting one of their conference topics. Encourage the children to share what they drew with their families.

Take turns, by class, rolling the Conference Cube. Note which speaker lands on the top, and have class members state something that individual spoke about in conference.

President James E. Faust

President Gordon B. Hinckley

President Thomas S. Monson

Image 4-1

5
How Are Our Lives Blessed When We Follow the Prophet?

PREPARATION: Print out or photocopy and cut apart the six quotes and their presentation suggestions.

Make a lift-a-flap page for each child. To do so, cut out the six prophet flaps and position them on top of the corresponding blessings. Tape the top of each flap to the blessing page.

One group will need a book. The Book of Mormon group will need a sack with some simple costumes, such as headbands, armbands, and/or robes. Arrange with the pianist and chorister to be familiar with the songs listed in the lesson.

PRESENTATION: Divide the children into six groups, each with an adult leader. Give each group a quote from President Gordon B. Hinckley. Allow the groups five minutes to discuss their topic and prepare a presentation for the Primary. (Quotes come from *Ensign,* June 2000, 18–21.)

ACTIVITY: When all the groups have presented their quotes, distribute the lift-a-flap pages. Read them with the children. Suggest that the children use their lift-a-flap page to teach a family home evening lesson.

Quote 1: "Believe in the Book of Mormon as another witness of the Son of God. . . . Let us

read it. Let us dwell upon its truths. Let us learn its message and be blessed accordingly."

Presentation suggestion: Read the quote. Assign the following parts:

Reader: When we read the Book of Mormon, we feel God's spirit. The book's heroes seem to be teaching us what we can do in our own lives.

Hero #1: I am Ammon. I trusted in the Lord that I could safely go on a mission to teach the very people who hated me. God helped me. He will help you fulfill your missions too.

Hero #2: I am Nephi. The Lord asked me to build a ship. I had never done that before. But I trusted that God would show me how. He did. You can trust the Lord too. He will show you how to accomplish even difficult things.

Hero #3: I am one of the children who Jesus blessed when he visited us in the land Bountiful. I felt his love. I know he loves you too. Let him bless your life.

Hero #4: I am Captain Moroni. I fought for the freedom of my people. It is important that we are all free to worship as we please in a safe land. Don't let anyone take away your freedom to choose. Be strong!

Hero #5: I am an Anti-Nephi-Lehi. I buried my

weapons in a hole. I chose not to fight anymore. You can choose not to fight anymore in your families and with your friends. Live in peace!

Quote 2: "You never need be ashamed of praying. Get on your knees as the day starts. Get on your knees as the day closes and offer prayer unto the Lord, and ask Him to bless you in dealing with your problems, to bless you in your schooling, bless you in all you do. . . . Don't forget to pray."

Presentation suggestion: Have someone read the quote, then act out the following situations, adding more, if needed. Afterward, have each of the children name one way that praying has blessed them or that a prayer was answered.

Child A: (Standing and wondering) I don't know what to say for my talk this Sunday. I will ask Heavenly Father to help me to know what to say in my talk.

Child B: (Standing and looking all around) I love my backyard. It is so beautiful. I will pray to Heavenly Father and thank him for all the beautiful flowers and trees that I have. They make me feel so happy.

Child C: (Standing nervously) I am worried that big bully Jeff will pick on me again today. I will ask Heavenly Father to help me know what to do if Jeff starts to push me around. I will also pray for Jeff to be happier and not want to fight.

Child D: My parents are so great to take me places. I'm glad I have them. I will pray to Heavenly Father and thank him for giving me a dad who takes me swimming and wants to play with me. I will also thank him for a mom who takes me shopping and reads with me.

Quote 3: "Get all the education that you can. The Lord has laid upon you a mandate [command] that you should learn, that you should study. . . . Be smart!"

Presentation suggestion: Have a child act out reading and writing and have the audience guess what he is doing. Read the prophet's quote. Have each child list a blessing that comes from learning. Sing the following words to the tune of "Book of Mormon Stories" (*Children's Songbook,* 118) and teach them to the entire group:

The prophet says to study

And so that is what I'll do.

I need to know about the world,

The stars, and planets, too.

A, B, C, D, E, F, G

And 2 + 2 is 4

I'll do my part

To be smart

And learn more!

Quote 4: "No boy or girl in this Church should become involved with the use of illegal drugs—not one. They don't need drugs. Drugs will destroy them."

Presentation suggestion: Read the quote. Have a child briefly explain the Word of Wisdom to the other children.

Invite everyone to stand and do jumping jacks, repeating together, "Our minds and bodies are healthy, because we don't do drugs!"

Quote 5: "I decry the filth, the rot, the violence, and the profanity that spew from television screens into our homes. . . . I feel sorry for children who do not learn the wonders to be found in good books."

Presentation suggestions: Read the quote. Pretend to be watching television. Get up and turn it off, saying, "I've watched enough TV today. I'll think I'll go read a book." Have each member of your group pretend to be reading as they share the names of their favorite books. Have the pianist play "Follow the Prophet" (*Children's Songbook,* 110) while the entire group passes a book around. When the music stops, have the children chant together: "Set your mind free. Turn off the TV!"

Quote 6: "We need to stand a little taller, be a little kinder, be a little better, each of us, than we have been."

Presentation suggestion: Read the quote. Have members of the group share an example of being kind to someone who is different from how they are. Use a variety of differences, such as religious, physical, cultural, and so on. Ask everyone to sing, "I'll Walk with You" (*Children's Songbook,* 140).

Image 5-1

Image 5-2

6

Through the Ages People Have Been Blessed As They Have Followed the Prophet

PREPARATION: Print out or make two copies of each of the match game cards. You will be arranging them on a bulletin board in a two-by-four grid. Turning over the cards will be easier if you punch a hole at the top of each card, tie a short string through the hole, and hang the cards on thumbtacks from their strings. Be familiar with the scriptures referenced in the activity.

PRESENTATION: Using the eight different pictures on the cards, tell the following stories about how obeying the prophets brings blessings and not listening to or obeying the prophets brings unhappiness. Then mix up all the cards and hang them in a grid pattern on the board. Have the children take turns trying to find the matching pictures. When a match is made, have the child briefly relate the corresponding story to see if she was listening.

MATCHING GAME STORIES: *Elijah* (1 Kings 17:8–16). Many people were starving. The prophet Elijah was hungry too. He asked a poor widow if she would feed him some bread. She told him she had only enough flour and oil to feed herself and her son. But she bravely obeyed Elijah. She fed him first and, to her surprise, every day she had more flour and oil in her barrels.

Enoch (Moses 6:21–7:69). Enoch preached repentance. Some of the people obeyed him. Enoch taught them the gospel, and they were baptized. They built a city called Zion. For many years Enoch urged them to be more like Jesus. The people grew strong and faithful. Jesus visited the city. Finally, Jesus took the whole city to heaven.

Elisha (2 Kings 5). Naaman, a leader of the Syrian army, had leprosy. It was a terrible disease that slowly caused death. Naaman's servant girl was an Israelite. She said the prophet could heal him. Naaman went to see the prophet Elisha. Elisha did not come out of his house to see Naaman. Instead, he sent his servant to tell Naaman to wash in the Jordan River seven times. Naaman was furious. He was an important man, and this Israelite prophet would not even come out to speak to him. Besides, the Jordan River was small and muddy. There were bigger rivers in his own country. He turned to go home. But his servants begged Naaman to do what the prophet had said. Finally, Naaman washed seven times in the Jordan River. His skin immediately became as clean and fresh as a baby's.

Samuel (Helaman 13–16; 3 Nephi 11). Five years before Jesus was born on the earth, the

21

prophet Samuel came to the wicked Nephites and told them to repent. Some of the people believed him. They repented and were baptized. They learned about Jesus. The Nephites who had repented, along with their children, were among those who did not die when Jesus came to visit the Americas after his resurrection.

Abinadi (Mosiah 11–17). King Noah was wicked. He was leading his people to sin. He was selfish and lazy. He made others do all the work. God sent Abinadi to teach the king and his people that there was a better way to live. Abinadi told them about Christ. He said they needed to repent and believe in the Savior. King Noah was angry and had Abinadi killed. But Alma, one of Noah's priests, believed Abinadi. Alma had tried to stop the king from hurting the prophet. But then the king tried to kill Alma. Alma escaped and wrote down the words of Abinadi. He taught others the truth. These people lived in peace. They shared what they had and did not fight. They were blessed with happiness.

Peter (Acts 5). The prophet Peter asked the Saints to sell their possessions and bring the money to the Apostles. The Apostles then would distribute to every person what they needed so there would be no poor. But a husband and wife, Ananias and Sapphira, only pretended to give everything. They secretly kept some of the money for themselves. Peter knew they were lying. He asked them why they had held back some of the money. Ananias and Sapphira had been caught and they died.

Lehi (1 Nephi 1, 2). The people of Jerusalem were wicked. God gave a man named Lehi a vision. In the vision was a book that said Jerusalem would be destroyed because the people would not repent. Lehi tried to warn the people to change before it was too late. Most of them laughed at him. Some even tried to kill him. God told Lehi to take his family and leave Jerusalem. Lehi's family followed him to a new land where they would be safe. Later, the Lord told Lehi that Jerusalem had been destroyed.

Daniel (Daniel 6). King Darius thought very highly of Daniel and often asked him about important matters of the kingdom. But King Darius's other servants were not righteous men like Daniel. They convinced the king to make a new law that no man could pray to God. If a man did pray, he would be cast into a den of lions. Because Daniel loved the Lord, he went into his house and prayed despite the new law. When the king's servants found Daniel, they threw him into a den with lions. This made the king sad because he loved Daniel. He was very worried about Daniel and thought that Daniel would be killed by the lions. King Darius went to the den and discovered that the Lord had blessed Daniel because of his obedience and shut the lions' mouths so they could not hurt him. The king then changed the law and commanded that his wicked servants be thrown in the lions' den for their disobedience.

Elijah (1 Kings 17:8–16)

Image 6-1

Enoch (Moses 6:21–7:69)

Image 6-2

Daniel (Daniel 6)

Image 6-3

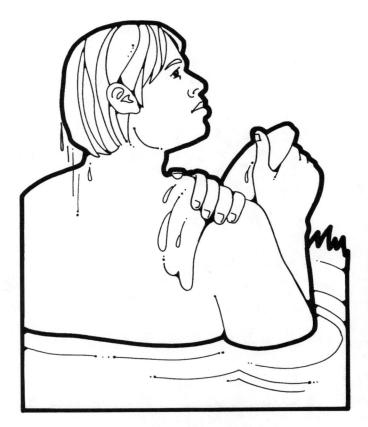

Elisha (2 Kings 5)

Image 6-4

Samuel (Helaman 13–16; 3 Nephi 11)

Image 6-5

Abinadi (Mosiah 11–17)

Image 6-6

Peter (Acts 5)

Image 6-7

Lehi (1 Nephi 1, 2)

Image 6-8

7
The True Church of Jesus Christ Was Restored through the Prophet Joseph Smith

PREPARATION: Be familiar with Joseph Smith—History in the Pearl of Great Price. Tape a picture of Joseph Smith on a plain box. Print out or photocopy, cut apart, and store the questions on the next page in the Joseph Smith box. On cardstock, copy a "Restoration Wheel" for each child. Attach the smaller circle to the top of the larger one with a paper fastener.

PRESENTATION: Show children the box with Joseph Smith's picture and briefly tell the Restoration story. Tell the children to follow along by using their "Restoration Wheels." Prompt them when it is time to turn the wheel.

RESTORATION STORY: (Before beginning the story, have the children turn their wheels to the picture numbered 1.) A fourteen-year-old boy named Joseph Smith wondered which church to join. He read in the Bible, "If any of you lack wisdom, let him ask of God" (James 1:5). He decided he would ask God which church to join.

He went to a small grove near his home and prayed.

(Turn the wheel to picture 2.) A bright light appeared over his head. He saw two personages. One, pointing to the other, said, Joseph, "This is My Beloved Son. Hear Him!" The Son told him not to join any church. Instead, as Joseph learned later, God would help him restore the true Church.

Joseph was so exhausted from the vision that he found himself weak and lying on his back. When he arose, he went back to his family's farm and told his mother he had learned for himself that the church they had been attending was not true.

(Turn the wheel to picture 3.) Three years later, Joseph was praying in bed. A personage in a robe appeared at his bedside, standing in the air. He radiated light. He said that his name was Moroni and that he would give Joseph gold plates to translate.

As Moroni was talking, Joseph saw a vision of the place where the plates were buried. He recognized a hill not far from his family's farm.

The next day, he went to the hill and moved a rock near the top of the hill, finding a stone box hidden under the rock. Inside the box were the plates. The angel again appeared and told him it was not time to remove the plates but that Joseph should meet Moroni at that same time and place each year.

(Turn the wheel to picture 4.) After four years, Joseph was allowed to take the plates home. Mean men tried to steal the plates. Joseph had to hide them in different places to keep them safe.

Heavenly Father helped Joseph to know what the writing said on the plates. Scribes wrote the words down. One of those scribes was Oliver Cowdery. Later, the words were published as the Book of Mormon.

(Turn the wheel to picture 5.) One day, John the Baptist came to Joseph and Oliver. He gave them the Aaronic Priesthood and told them to baptize each other.

Peter, James, and John came later and gave Joseph and Oliver the Melchizedek Priesthood. They ordained Joseph and Oliver to be Apostles—special witnesses of Christ.

(Turn the wheel to picture 6.) In April 1830 the early Saints held the first meeting of the restored Church. They prayed and partook of the sacrament. Joseph and Oliver blessed four men that they might receive the gift of the Holy Ghost. They gave some men the priesthood. The true Church of Jesus Christ had been restored.

ACTIVITY: Invite the children to pull a question from the Joseph Smith box. Read the question and ask the child to answer it by using the "Restoration Wheel."

For singing time, ask the chorister to have the children sing the following songs from the *Children's Songbook:* "On a Golden Springtime," verse 3 (88); "The Golden Plates" (86); "The Priesthood Is Restored" (89); "This Is My Beloved Son," verse 3 (76); and "The Church of Jesus Christ" (77).

How old was Joseph Smith when he experienced the First Vision?
What scripture motivated Joseph Smith to pray in the Sacred Grove?
What question did Joseph ask Heavenly Father?
Who answered Joseph's question?
Which church did Jesus tell Joseph to join?
Who appeared to Joseph after he prayed in bed?
How many years passed between the time Joseph first saw the plates and the time when he was allowed to take the plates home?
Where did Joseph find the golden plates?
Why did Joseph have to keep hiding the plates?
Who gave Joseph and Oliver Cowdery the Aaronic Priesthood?
Who gave Joseph and Oliver the Melchizedek Priesthood?

Image 7-1

Image 7-2

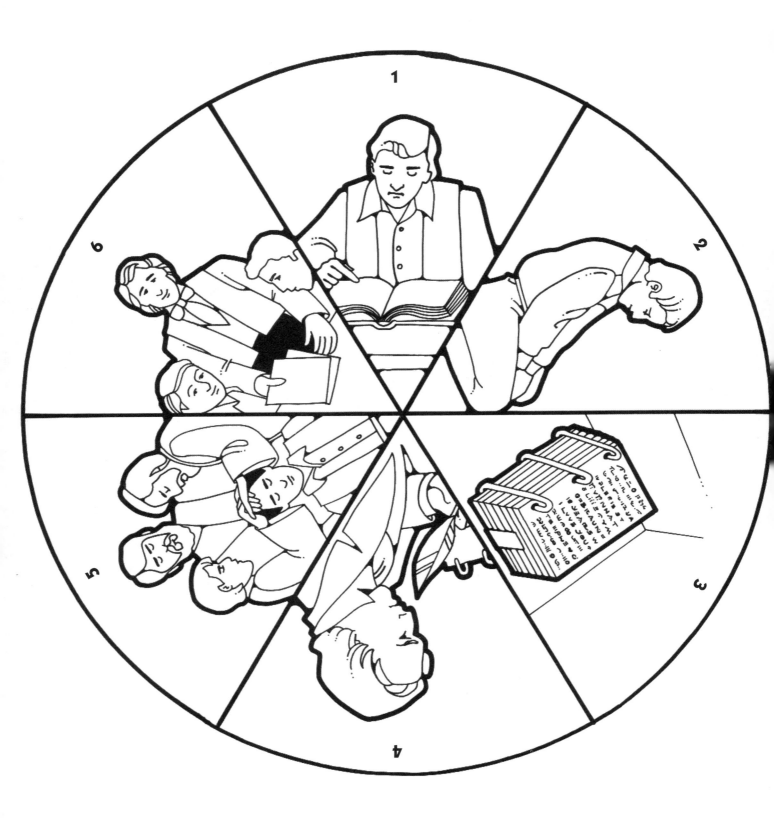

Image 7-3

8
Heavenly Father Sends Prophets to Warn and Teach His Children

PREPARATION: Be familiar with the scriptures referred to in the activity. Enlarge the board game grid to poster size. Laminate it. Print out or photocopy, cut apart, and stack the cards. Print out or photo-copy, color, cut out, and laminate the game token. Put masking tape on the back of the game token. Gather small soft items, such as beanbags or stuffed animals, and a blindfold. Set up a large easel in the front of the room. You will also need one die or a spinner.

PRESENTATION: Ask an older child who understands directions to take off her shoes and stand on the opposite side of the room from the picture of Christ. Ask the other children to pay close attention as you blindfold the child and then spread the small items across the floor. Invite the blindfolded child to walk slowly from one side of the room to the picture of Christ. Tell her that there are several obstacles in her way. To help the "blind" child ask another older child to give directions, warning her about the objects until she reaches the other side.

Explain that we are like the "blind" child. We cannot see the problems the world may face in the future. A prophet is like the child who gave the directions. Through the spirit of prophecy, the prophet can "see" what dangers lie ahead.

He warns us of those dangers. We will be safe if we follow the directions the prophet gives us. The prophet will lead us back to Christ.

ACTIVITY: Display the board game. Before starting the game, tell the children about some of the less familiar prophets listed below. Then, using the die or the spinner, take turns moving the token the amount of spaces rolled. Make sure you go the direction of the arrows when moving forward and the opposite direction when moving backward. Follow the instructions on both the board and the cards. Rather than competing, have the whole group play together as a team to reach the end.

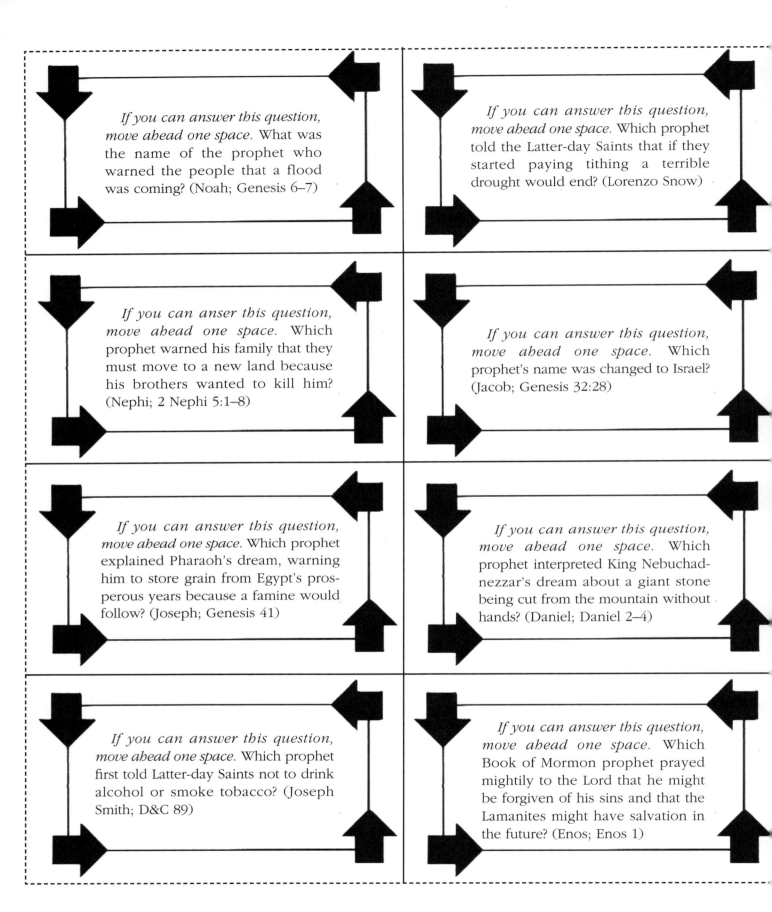

If you can answer this question, move ahead one space. What was the name of the prophet who warned the people that a flood was coming? (Noah; Genesis 6–7)

If you can answer this question, move ahead one space. Which prophet told the Latter-day Saints that if they started paying tithing a terrible drought would end? (Lorenzo Snow)

If you can anser this question, move ahead one space. Which prophet warned his family that they must move to a new land because his brothers wanted to kill him? (Nephi; 2 Nephi 5:1–8)

If you can answer this question, move ahead one space. Which prophet's name was changed to Israel? (Jacob; Genesis 32:28)

If you can answer this question, move ahead one space. Which prophet explained Pharaoh's dream, warning him to store grain from Egypt's prosperous years because a famine would follow? (Joseph; Genesis 41)

If you can answer this question, move ahead one space. Which prophet interpreted King Nebuchadnezzar's dream about a giant stone being cut from the mountain without hands? (Daniel; Daniel 2–4)

If you can answer this question, move ahead one space. Which prophet first told Latter-day Saints not to drink alcohol or smoke tobacco? (Joseph Smith; D&C 89)

If you can answer this question, move ahead one space. Which Book of Mormon prophet prayed mightily to the Lord that he might be forgiven of his sins and that the Lamanites might have salvation in the future? (Enos; Enos 1)

Image 8-1a

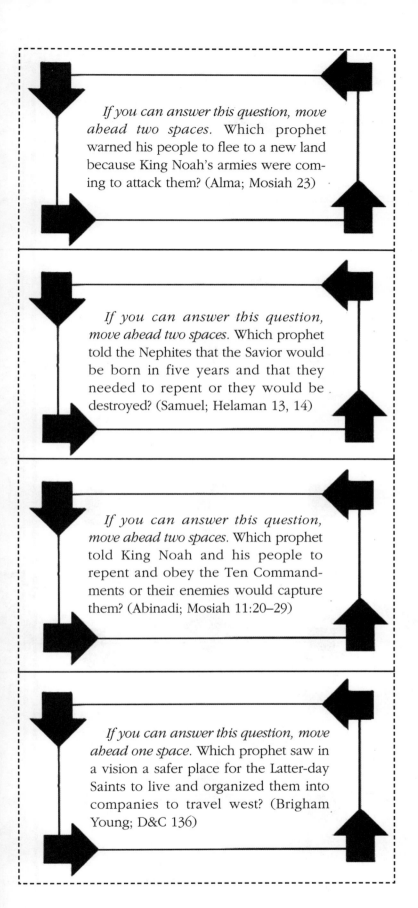

If you can answer this question, move ahead two spaces. Which prophet warned his people to flee to a new land because King Noah's armies were coming to attack them? (Alma; Mosiah 23)

If you can answer this question, move ahead two spaces. Which prophet told the Nephites that the Savior would be born in five years and that they needed to repent or they would be destroyed? (Samuel; Helaman 13, 14)

If you can answer this question, move ahead two spaces. Which prophet told King Noah and his people to repent and obey the Ten Commandments or their enemies would capture them? (Abinadi; Mosiah 11:20–29)

If you can answer this question, move ahead one space. Which prophet saw in a vision a safer place for the Latter-day Saints to live and organized them into companies to travel west? (Brigham Young; D&C 136)

Image 8-1b

GAME TOKEN

Image 8-2

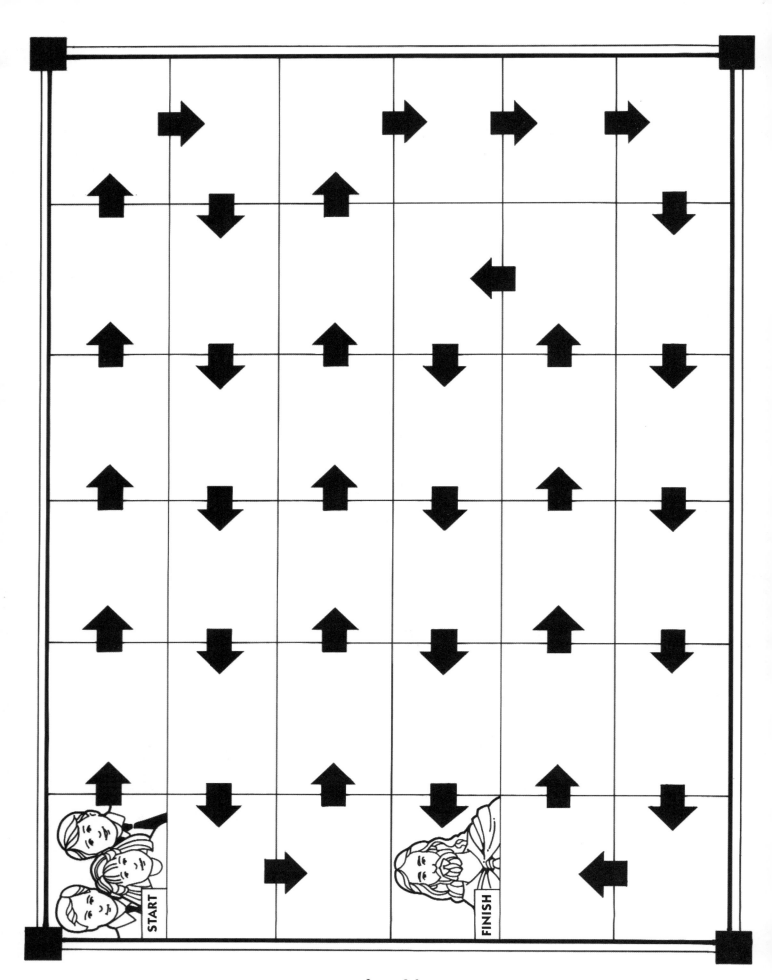

Image 8-3

9

How Can We Follow the Prophet?

PREPARATION: Print out or photocopy, color, and cut out the hikers. Draw a hillside on a large section of cardboard (see diagram). Poke a hole at the top of the hill and at the bottom. Thread a string through the front two holes and tie it in the back. Tape the taller hiker to the string in the front. Display the cardboard on an easel in the front of the room.

PRESENTATION: Using the poster and figures, tell and act out the following story. (Slowly pull the string to make the older sister hike. Hold the other figure so she can go off the path and fall.)

Two sisters, Ashley and Amanda, went hiking at a national park. Before they started, the ranger insisted on giving them a little speech. Amanda was too excited to pay much attention. She had heard there was a lake at the top, and she planned on swimming there. She paced back and forth. "Come on," she said. "Let's go, before it gets too hot!"

"OK," said the ranger, "you can go now, but be careful."

The trail was easy at first. Amanda ran on ahead.

"Slow down!" Ashley called. "The ranger said not to run."

But Amanda kept on hurrying.

When they got about halfway up the mountain, Amanda started getting thirsty. It was hot and dusty. She sat on a rock and saw how far she still had to go. She sighed. This was harder than she had expected.

Then she saw a space between some trees. She figured she could take a shortcut through those trees to the trail above. It looked steep, but she had on her new hiking boots.

Grabbing tall weeds, she pulled herself up the steep slope. But then the dirt floor turned into slippery rock, and she started sliding. She tried to grab a branch but she missed and went tumbling down the hill.

Her ankle hit against a stump and landed in a strange, twisted position. Boy, did it hurt! Suddenly Amanda felt panicked. She was hot, tired, and in pain. She started to cry. Everything was ruined! Now she would not get to swim in the lake.

After what seemed like forever, Ashley came walking around the bend. Surprised, she called, "Amanda! What happened?"

33

"I fell down the hill," Amanda sobbed. "I'm thirsty. Can I have some of your water?"

"You can have a little sip," Ashley offered. "But I don't have much left. We've got to get some help for you."

Later, as Amanda was sitting in the first-aid station, Ashley asked her how she had fallen. Amanda told her she was in a hurry and had run the first half. But running had made her hot and tired. So she had tried to take a shortcut off the trail and had fallen.

"Weren't you listening to anything the ranger told us?" Ashley asked. "He said this time of year gets very hot. You should never run or go off the trail. You should always take plenty of water. And you didn't take any water at all."

"I don't remember the ranger saying those things. I guess I wasn't listening. I'm sorry I ruined our plans," said Amanda.

Why did Amanda fall? What might have happened had Amanda listened to the ranger? Did Ashley *listen* to the ranger? Did Ashley *trust* the ranger? Did she *follow* his advice?

A prophet is like the ranger. Like Ashley, we have to *listen to, trust,* and *follow* his advice. Otherwise, like Amanda did physically, we might spiritually fall and experience pain. The prophet wants us to be happy. He helps us avoid unnecessary suffering.

ACTIVITY: Play "Simon Says." Have the children line up in the back of the room. One child should come to the front and pretend to be Simon. Have the child say things such as: "Simon says take two baby steps forward . . . Simon says take four scissor hops to the side . . . Simon says take one giant step backward . . . Simon says hop three times forward." If the child does not say, "Simon says . . ." the other children should not follow the directions. If a child does follow the directions when this has not been said, that child must move to the back of the room. The first child to reach "Simon" gets to give the directions.

After the game, explain that when we follow the prophet's directions we are able to move forward. When we disobey or do something without guidance, we fall behind.

Ask the children what our prophet has asked us to do recently that will help us be happier.

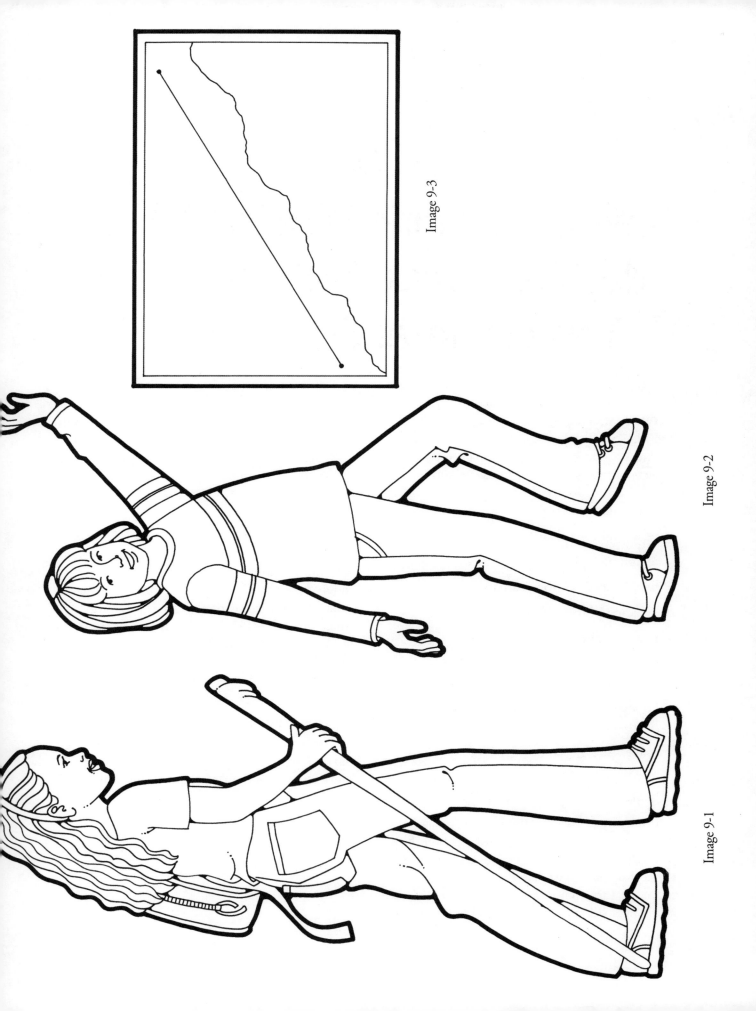

Image 9-3

Image 9-2

Image 9-1

10

What Specific Direction Has the Prophet Given Us During This General Conference?

PREPARATION: Take notes during the First Presidency's and the Apostles' talks during conference. Circle keywords and main topics. Find objects to represent ten or twelve of those topics and hide the objects in a pillowcase. Topics/objects might include:

repentance—a cleanser or eraser

temples—a picture of a temple

the Word of Wisdom—an apple

avoiding pornography—a good video

paying tithing—coins or a bank

trying to be like Jesus—a picture of the Savior

honesty—a test from school, or a broken object

prayer—a figurine or picture of someone praying

being a good example—a candle

Print out or photocopy and cut out a set of mobile pieces for each child. Punch holes through the dots at the top. Tie different lengths of yarn to the holes. Tie the other ends of the pieces of yarn to a foot-long dowel or stick. Tie one longer string to the center top of the stick (to hang it from the ceiling). Bring crayons and pens. You may also want to send home a note with the children prior to conference. In the note, mention topics the children should listen for and remember.

PRESENTATION: Have a few children lightly touch the full pillowcase. Tell them you have some objects that represent the themes spoken of during conference. Can they guess what they might be? Let them guess, and pull out the items that they guess correctly. Ask the children to retell what the General Authority spoke of in his address. Continue reviewing the topics until all the objects have been pulled out of the bag. (If they have a hard time guessing topics, give them hints.)

ACTIVITY: Distribute the mobiles and crayons. Ask the children to choose their four favorite topics from those you just discussed and draw corresponding pictures on the four blank mobile pieces. Older children can use the pens to write key words on each piece. Encourage them to hang their mobiles in their rooms for the next six months to remind them of what our leaders have asked us to do.

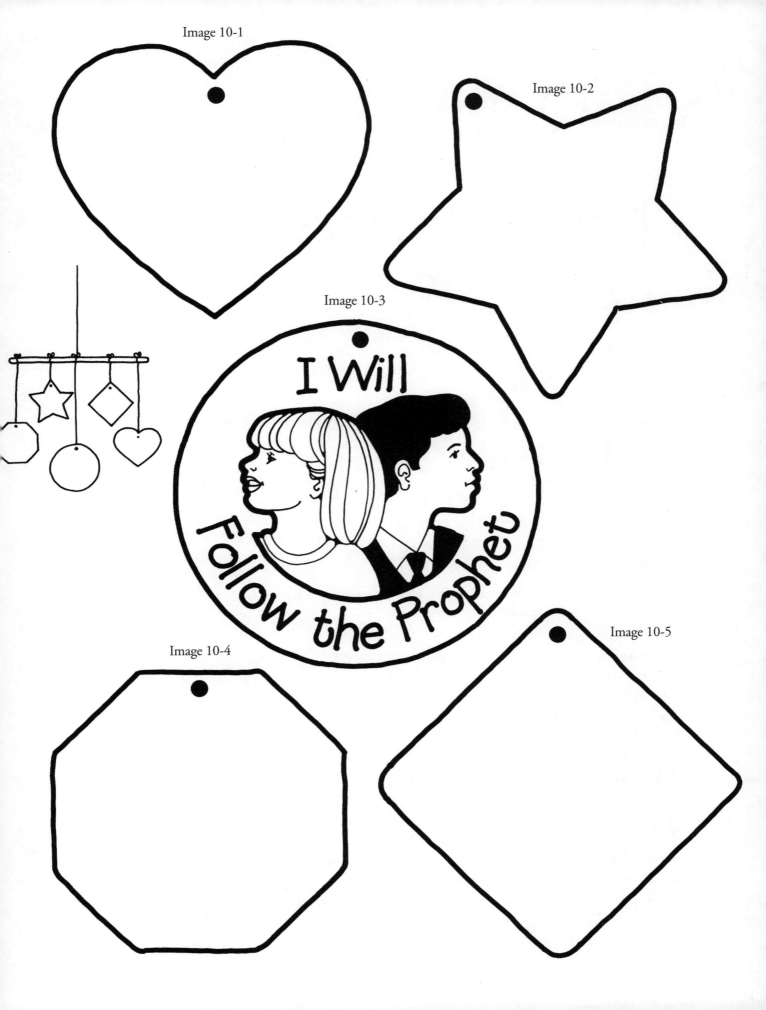

Image 10-1

Image 10-2

Image 10-3

I Will Follow the Prophet

Image 10-4

Image 10-5

11
Prophets Prophesy of Things to Come

PREPARATION: Print out, photocopy, color, cut out, and laminate the "What's Missing?" figures. Put masking tape on the backs of the figures. Arrange them on a flannel board or laminated board and display the board on a large easel in the front of the room. Bring a tablecloth to cover the board.

PRESENTATION: Tell the following stories of prophets, pointing out the corresponding figures.

Suggest that the children listen carefully, since they will need to repeat the stories during the game.

ACTIVITY: After telling all the stories, play "What's Missing?" by covering the board with the tablecloth. Remove one of the figures. Ask the children to guess which piece you removed. When they guess correctly, they must retell the story of the prophecy.

FIGURES WITH STORIES: *Malachi* (Malachi 4:5–6; D&C 110:13–16). Malachi prophesied that before Christ's Second Coming, Elijah would return and turn the hearts of children to their fathers. More than two thousand years later, Elijah appeared to Joseph Smith and Oliver Cowdery in the Kirtland Temple. He gave them priesthood power to seal families together forever.

Moses (Exodus 7–14). The children of Israel were slaves to the Egyptians. Moses warned the Pharaoh of impending disaster if he did not let the Israelites go. Each time Moses prophesied of a new plague, it came true. First, the river turned to blood, killing all the fish in it. Next came swarms of frogs, lice, and flies. Diseases soon killed the Egyptians' animals. Then a disease caused sores to break out on the Egyptians' skin. Next, hail destroyed their crops. Locusts ate what was left. Then they experienced three days of darkness. Finally, all firstborn Egyptian sons died. After Pharaoh's own son died, he let Moses and the Israelites go.

Abinadi (Mosiah 17:9-20). Wicked king Noah and his priests were angry about the words of the prophet Abinadi. They burned Abinadi to death. As he was dying, Abinadi prophesied that his killers would die the same type of death. Later, king Noah's own men caused his death by fire.

The Present-day First Presidency ("The Family: A Proclamation to the World"). In 1995, the First Presidency and Council of the Twelve Apostles warned all individuals, communities, and nations that calamities would be brought upon those who do not support and strengthen marriages and families.

Jonah (Jonah 1–3). The Lord asked the prophet Jonah to go to the wicked city of Nineveh and tell the people to repent. Jonah was fearful and ran away instead of going into Nineveh. But the Lord had prepared a way for Jonah to learn that he would be protected if he were obedient. Jonah was cast into the belly of a whale for three days, where he prayed to the Lord for help. The Lord allowed Jonah to return to dry land and then asked him to preach to the city of Nineveh. Jonah obeyed the Lord and prophesied to the people that their great city would be overthrown in forty days if they did not repent. The people of Nineveh believed Jonah. They repented of their sins, and the Lord preserved them.

Nephi (1 Nephi 12–15). Nephi received a prophecy that the Spirit of God would guide many white men to sail across the ocean to the place where the Nephites and Lamanites lived. These new people would take over the land. This happened two thousand years later when Christopher Columbus sailed to the Americas, and when many others followed him to live in America.

Joseph Smith (D&C 1:23). God told Joseph Smith that the fulness of the gospel would someday be preached to the ends of the world. This has not been completely fulfilled yet. But it is exciting to know that every country will have a chance to hear the missionaries someday.

Alma (Alma 30:48-50). Korihor ridiculed the people who believed in Christ. He told people there was no Christ. Alma prophesied that Korihor would not be able to speak. As soon as Alma said these words, Korihor could not speak.

Malachi (Malachi 4:5–6; D&C 110:13–16

Image 11-1

Moses (Exodus 7–14)

Image 11-2

Alma (Alma 30:48–50)

Image 11-3

Nephi (1 Nephi 12–15)

Image 11-4

Joseph Smith (D&C 1:23)

Image 11-5

Jonah (Jonah 1–3)

Image 11-6

The Family: A Proclamation to the World

Image 11-7

Abinadi (Mosiah 17:9–20)

Image 11-8

12
Prophets Have Prophesied of the First and Second Comings of Jesus Christ

PREPARATION: Enlarge the nativity picture adn the puzzle pieces. Glue the puzzle pieces to the back of the picture and cut apart. Put masking tape on the back of each piece and hide the pieces around the room. Set up a display board in the front. Bring a blank piece of paper and crayons for each child. Arrange with the pianist and chorister to sing "When He Comes Again" (*Children's Songbook,* 82).

PRESENTATION: Explain that many years before Christ's birth, prophets taught that a Savior would come into the world. Ever since Christ's crucifixion, prophets have taught us that he will come again. Each prophecy is like a piece of a puzzle. When we put all the pieces together, we have a better understanding of the Savior's mission before he came to earth, while he walked among men, and after his Resurrection.

ACTIVITY: Invite children to find a puzzle piece, read what is on the back, and post it on the board.

Distribute the paper and crayons. Invite the children to draw what they think the earth will be like when Jesus comes again. Ask everyone to sing, "When He Comes Again." As you are singing, point to the classes, one at a time. Have them stand and show their illustrations to the entire group.

Image 12-1

Image 12-2